MW01088275

THE Christ Child

Also by

Adam S. Miller

Letters to a Young Mormon

An Early Resurrection

Original Grace

with Rosalynde F. Welch

Seven Gospels

Seven Visions

THE Christ Child

ADAM S. MILLER

Visit us at DeseretBook.com

Library of Congress Cataloging-in-Publication Data

CIP data on file
ISBN 978-1-63993-338-9

Printed in the United States of America
PubLitho, Draper, UT

10 9 8 7 6 5 4 3 2 1

For Mom

Contents

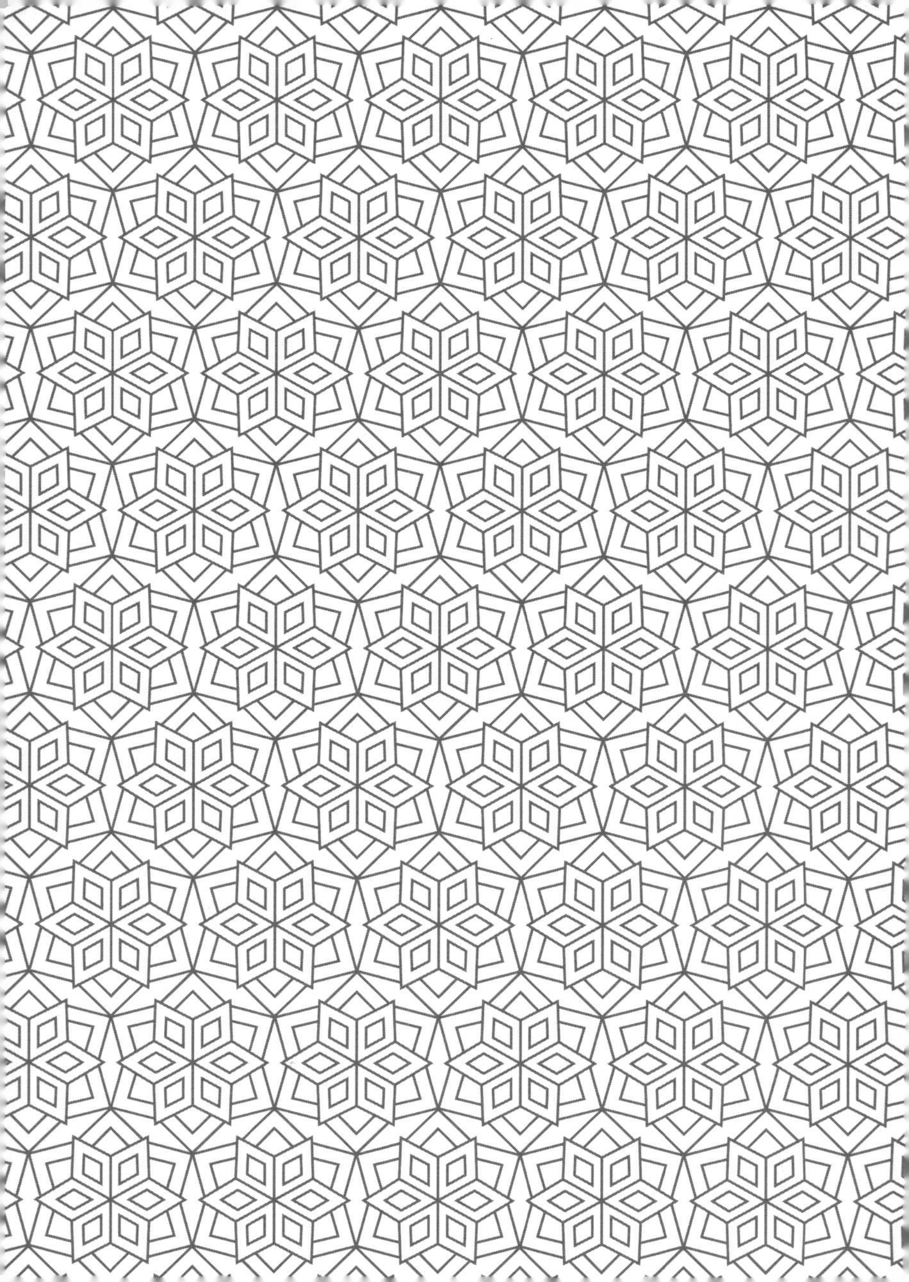

Introduction

In the photo, I'm a child. It's Christmas.

I'm kneeling on the floor, holding up a gift, a jet or a helicopter, to show the photographer, probably my dad. A mound of shucked wrapping paper is piled next to me. I'm wearing baby blue pajamas with matching top and bottoms. The sleeves are a little short and the knees are worn white. My hair is still fine and straight, bangs level with my eyebrows.

On the back of the photo, my mother's handwriting says it's 1984.

I'm eight years old.

My mother is also in the photo, together with my older brother and sister. We're in the living room of our farmhouse. Everything is rural Pennsylvania, rolling hills and country roads. I've never even seen a suburb. The living room walls are off-white. The carpet is dappled brown and orange. The front door is directly behind me, a different shade of white, two panes of glass. A cardboard wreath fashioned from the rim of a paper plate hangs on the door. There's snow outside. The old house is a sieve and cold air leaches under that door.

My mother is sitting on the floor beside me, to my right, a little behind. She's young. Her short hair is still dark brown. All twenty volumes of our Encyclopedia Britannica are displayed behind her. She's wearing a red sweater and dark jeans, already dressed for the day. Her cheeks are a little rosy. She's got a pink Care Bear on her lap. A rainbow arches across its belly. She's looking past me, probably at my sister, probably at the hole in the knee of her corduroys.

If I'm eight, then my sister is thirteen. She's sitting with her knees drawn up in front of her, leaning back against my brother's beanbag. She's wearing a blue sweater and fuzzy slippers. Lots of freckles. Instead of hugging her knees, she's hugging a chimpanzee. This stuffed animal is mine. Her name is Ruth. Rather than looking at me or anyone else, my sister—like any respectable teenager on Christmas morning—is staring off into the middle distance with a faint look of longing. The Game of Life, still wrapped in cellophane, is propped up next to her.

My brother lounges behind her in his beanbag. If I'm eight, he's fifteen. He has the independent air of someone presiding, willing and benevolent but at a remove. His brown hair sweeps across his forehead, parted from the left. He's wearing glasses, a blue shirt, faded blue jeans, white socks. A pile of boxes is stacked on the chair behind him. A beautiful woman in a daring white dress peeks out from behind the boxes, printed on an album cover. Or maybe a calendar. I don't remember my brother ever playing records, just cassettes. But I don't know how else this woman would be in the photo. My brother's jeans have a matching rip in their right knee. I doubt this rip is on purpose, but it might be cool. He's the only one in the picture looking right at me.

Or, maybe not.

My little sister, I find, has been hiding, Waldo-like, in the border of the photo. On the very edge of the bottom-right corner there's a sidelong flash of bangs, an oblique pinch of nose, the suggestion of an eyebrow. Just a hint of her. If I'm eight, she's six, the only real child in the photo. Already at eight, I'm no longer quite a child. I'm no longer (simply) innocent. I'm accountable. I've already ingested enough words and stories to change the substance of what I am—to alter, fundamentally, the chemistry of what I can see or want or do in the world.

In this photo, though, I'm still smiling. I look happy.

I'm clearly proud to display the gift. I look like I'm already imagining, as any child would, the games I'm going to play.

It's Christmas.

Christmas, everyone knows, is a holiday for children. This is its magic.

It's the day we celebrate the fact that, as Abinadi put it, "God himself" chose to "come down among the children of men" and join us by becoming a child (Mosiah 15:1).

At Christmas, we celebrate the fact that God became a baby.

Ten fingers and ten toes? I assume. Five or six pounds of flesh and bone, dimples, a shock of dark hair, eyes squeezed shut, already hungry, sucking his thumb? I imagine.

And all this—God as baby, Christ as child—is pivotal to "the great plan of the Eternal God" (Alma 34:9). This, somehow, is how God sets in motion his wild plan to save us.

I have another memory from this same Christmas. This memory comes from much earlier that morning. There is no photo. It happened, perhaps entirely, inside my own head.

I'd only recently been given my own room. It took years to renovate the upstairs of the farmhouse. Until then, I'd shared a room with my brother. Bunk beds. At night, after the lights were out, he would reach up from the bottom bunk, grab the edge of my blankets, and slowly—very slowly—pull them down through the crack between the wall and the bed frame, trying not to laugh.

I missed sharing a room. So we established a tradition that on special occasions, like Christmas Eve, I could come back. I could camp out with a pile of blankets on his bedroom floor. I could tuck myself under his window, between his closet and his bookshelves, next to the heating vent.

That Christmas morning, I remember waking up early, too early, excited for the day. And I remember wanting—keenly—to believe in the magic of Christmas.

It was still dark. The heat hadn't kicked on yet and the house was cold. I stayed burrowed in my blankets, waiting, listening. I listened to the winter wind rattle the window. I listened to my brother snoring. I listened to the old house creaking. I listened to my heart beating. I wondered how early it really was. I wondered if Santa had already come. I wondered if Santa could possibly be real. And then, layered into this silence, I heard something like the distant sound of sleigh bells.

This memory is strong and clear—not, really, the memory of those faint bells, but my memory of the whole train of thoughts and feelings that followed. The memory of me, like a grown-up, catching myself in the act.

Immediately, I doubted what I'd heard. I doubted the sleigh bells were real. Immediately, I strongly suspected that I was trying to manufacture something special and magical for myself, that I was kidding myself. And then immediately—and this is what's really stuck with me all these years—I felt bad about doubting Christmas and, so, *willed* myself to believe that there really had been bells, that I really had heard them, and that those faint bells really might be good evidence that Santa was real, good evidence that my faith in the magic of Christmas was, as a whole, warranted.

Christmas, though, doesn't work this way.

Christmas isn't just a reminder that God came as a child to save me. It's a clue to *how* God, in his coming, saves me.

Our celebrations of Christ's birth rightly emphasize "the condescension of God" (1 Nephi 11:16). They emphasize the miracle of someone fully divine not only coming to us, but becoming one of the smallest and most vulnerable among us.

What, after all, could be further from "the Lord Omnipotent" than a newborn baby? (Mosiah 3:5).

But, at the same time, what could better reveal the divine potential of even ordinary people than a baby?

To this end, Christ himself warns that, "except ye be converted, and become as little children, ye shall not enter into the kingdom of heaven" (Matthew 18:3). To be converted is to become again like a little child. "Suffer the little children to come unto me," Jesus commands, "for of such is the kingdom of God," and "whosoever shall not receive the kingdom of God as a little child, he shall not enter therein" (Mark 10:14–15). Or as Benjamin explains it, if I want to become "a saint through the atonement of Christ the Lord," I must become "as a child, submissive, meek, humble, patient, full of love, willing to submit to all things" (Mosiah 3:19).

In this way, Christ's arrival as a baby not only dramatically displays the miracle of his condescension, it quietly embodies something crucial about what I must also become in order to be saved.

Christ became a child to save me.

But to be saved by Christ, I too must become a child again.

This, I think, is what I—roughly, gropingly—sensed in the dark that cold Christmas morning. Something essential was slipping through my fingers. Something that, as a child, I'd taken for granted and naively enjoyed. Something that now, already at the age of eight, I felt anxious to recapture.

And feeling this way, I wasn't wrong. To be saved, this *is* what I need. I need, like a child, to trust and believe again. I need, like a child, to be creative and pliable again. I need, like a child, to be vulnerable and generous again.

The problem is that these aren't qualities I can will myself to have. Children don't *will* themselves into childlike states of awe, creativity, and openness. Children just are this way. These spontaneous qualities can't be forced. They come as gifts or, regardless of how I chase them, they're lost for good. Otherwise, I'm just kidding myself.

But if I can't will myself—like an adult would—into being a child again, how is it done?

This is a mystery. In fact, it's what Jesus calls *the* "mystery of the kingdom of God" (Mark 4:11). To join Jesus in his kingdom I must be initiated into this mystery. I must learn this secret. I must become a child again. Jesus must give me a new "heart to perceive," and new "eyes to see, and ears to hear" (Deuteronomy 29:4).

To join Jesus in his kingdom, I must—like Jesus—be born all over again.

When Nicodemus, an exemplary adult, comes "to Jesus by night," he wants to ask about the astonishing miracles Jesus has been performing (John 3:2). He doesn't see how they're possible. "No man can do these miracles," he tells Jesus (John 3:2).

But this topic doesn't interest Jesus. Jesus insists, instead, on talking about Christmas.

"Jesus answered and said unto him, Verily, verily, I say unto thee, Except a man be born again, he cannot see the kingdom of God" (John 3:3).

Nicodemus, an elder in Israel, is confused by this teaching. "How can a man be born when he is old? can he enter the second time into his mother's womb, and be born?" (John 3:4).

Nicodemus, perhaps despite himself, has asked the right question. And when it comes to seeing and entering the kingdom of God, this is the only question that matters. This is the exact question I must ask myself again and again.

How? How can I be born again when I'm already old?

How can a man like me—settled for decades into deep ruts of routine and suspicion, closing hard on fifty, a father whose own children are already grown—become a child again?

How could it be anything other than too late for me?

Jesus, somehow, is both God and man. He knows *everything*—but, still, he has the mind of a child. He is both the parent and the child. He is both the Father and the Son, "the Father, because he was conceived by the power of God; and the Son, because of the flesh; thus becoming the Father and Son" (Mosiah 15:3). He is wise like a serpent, and yet harmless like a dove (see Matthew 10:16).

This is the mystery of godliness: how to be both. How to become an adult, tempered by age and experience, and, nonetheless, see the world through a child's eyes.

The kingdom of God is hidden in plain sight. To see it, I just have to see the world as Christ sees it. I have to see the world through his childlike eyes, through the eyes of the Son.

Or to see the kingdom of God, I must, as Paul says, come to share "the mind of Christ" (1 Corinthians 2:16). This mind—Christ's mind—is full of awe and wonder. This mind is open and creative. This mind is vulnerable and full of love. This mind is the mind of a child.

The mind of Christ is the mind of a child.

To see the world through a child's eyes is to glimpse the mind of God.

"The younger children are," Alison Gopnik, professor of psychology at UC Berkely, writes, "the more mysterious they are."[1] From the perspective of neuroscience, "children aren't just defective adults, primitive grown-ups gradually attaining our perfection and complexity. Instead, children and adults are different forms of *Homo sapiens*."[2]

Children aren't just little adults. Children are a fundamentally different *kind* of human being. They inhabit a different form of life. Their brains work differently than ours and because "children's brains are radically different from ours, so their experience must be too."[3]

How is a child's brain different? "Psychologists and neuroscientists have discovered that babies not only learn more, but imagine more, care more, and experience more than we would have thought possible" and, in many ways, "young children are actually smarter, more imaginative, more caring, and even more conscious than adults are."[4]

Children are more conscious than adults. Children are wide

awake. Their minds are open rather than closed, big rather than small, soft rather than hard, plastic rather than rigid.

The mind of a child is childlike because it can *change*.

A child's mind is like a bird. Light on its feet, it trusts rather than worries. "Behold the fowls of the air: for they sow not, neither do they reap . . . ; yet your heavenly Father feedeth them" (Matthew 6:26).

A child's mind is like a flower. Pushing toward the sun, it plays rather than works. "Consider the lilies of the field, how they grow; they toil not, neither do they spin" (Matthew 6:28).

A child's mind is like an eye. Wide open, it sees rather than despises. "If therefore thine eye be single, thy whole body shall be full of light" (Matthew 6:22).

A child's mind is like a servant. Attentive, it's single rather than split. "No man can serve two masters: for either he will hate the one, and love the other; or else he will hold to the one, and despise the other" (Matthew 6:24).

Like the fowls of the air and the lilies of the field, a child's mind is trusting, playful, open, and single.

"Take therefore no thought for the morrow," Jesus says, "for the morrow shall take thought for the things of itself" (Matthew 6:34). This is the mind of a child.

Measured by the wisdom of this world, this mind is foolishness. It's mad. It's juvenile. It's irrational. It's irresponsible.

But to us, this mind is the salvation of God. "Unto us which are saved it is the power of God" because "the foolishness of God is wiser than men; and the weakness of God is stronger than men" (1 Corinthians 1:18, 25).

In the end, this may be the only dependable gauge of conversion, the only honest measure of whether I'm filled with Spirit and have begun a new life in Christ: when I opened my eyes this morning, did I see the world with a child's eyes?

This is Christmas: God becomes a baby. Christ becomes a child. And those who are wise travel however far they must to kneel in wonder and worship—like children—at the Christ Child's feet.

Have I seen the kingdom of God? Have I been converted? Do I have the mind of a child?

Do I believe in Christmas?

And if I had again the mind of a child—if I truly shared the mind of Christ—what could I see, what could I think, what could I do?

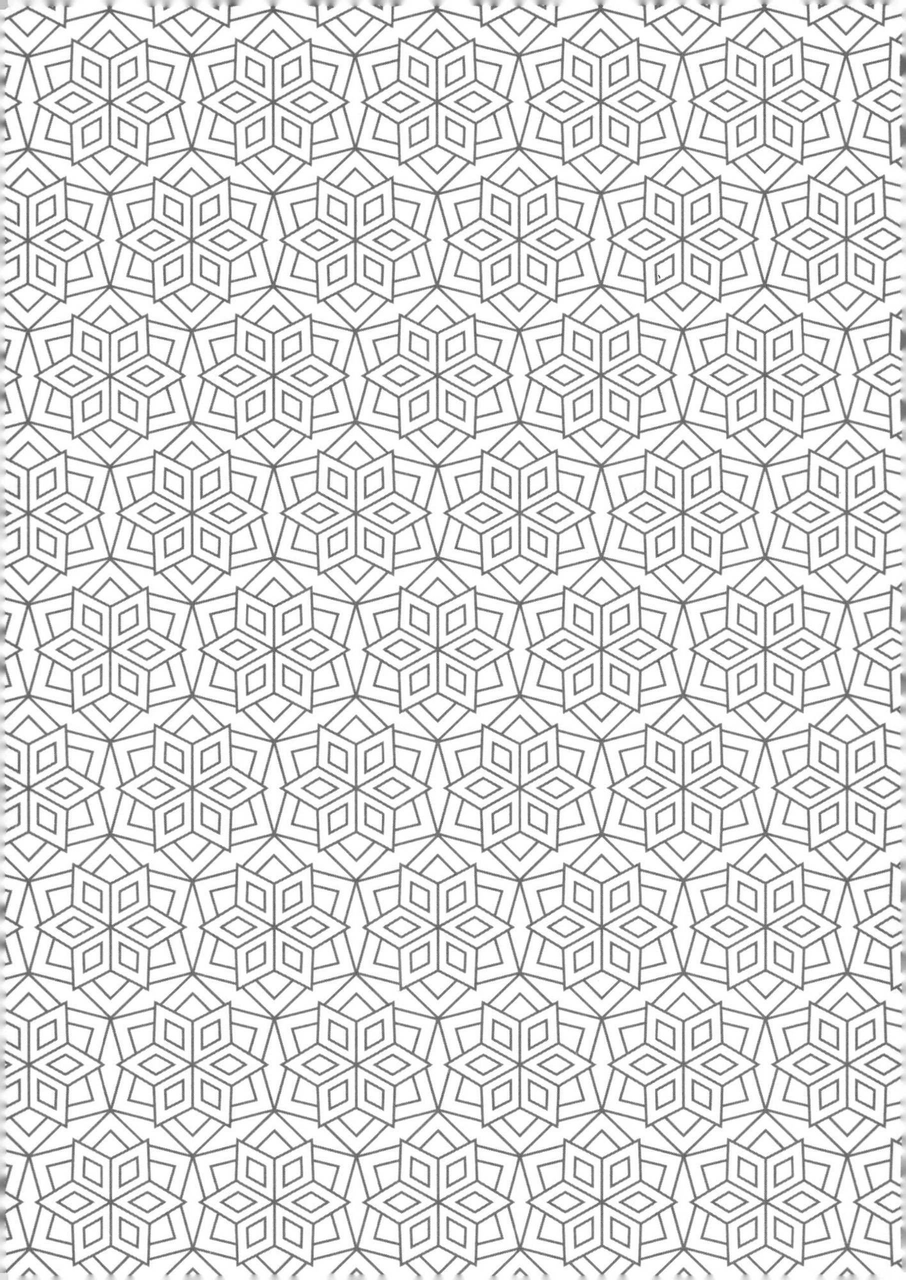

CHAPTER ONE

Awe

In the photo, I'm a father. It's Christmas.

I'm sitting on the floor, legs crossed. In the foreground, posing for the photographer, our daughter struggles to show her brother a giant box of blocks. A baby is crawling toward them. The photographer is, doubtless, my wife. From behind our daughter, I'm reaching to help. I'm wearing a black pullover and square, dark-rimmed glasses. My hair is short and frizzy—or curly, depending on how generous you feel. My pajama bottoms are navy and plaid. Everyone's pajamas are navy and plaid. We've got matching pajamas. This wasn't my idea, but I don't mind. No one is dressed for the day, not even our photographer.

A dot matrix code stamped on the back of the photo says 17 March 2007, so the picture itself is from 2006. This fits with the obvious age of the baby.

I'm thirty years old.

We're in the living room of a rented duplex in the suburbs of Dallas. Everything is baked clay and steeply pitched houses stretching across once-open plains. The living room walls are beige. The carpet is beige. I'm at the far left of the photo, with the Christmas tree in the corner behind me. The tree is real. We cut it down ourselves. The lights are colored, not white, and every identifiable ornament is a craft of some kind—a yellow cardboard star my wife made as a child, a laminated snowflake, a Christmas tree glued together from popsicle sticks, a picture of Jesus cut from a magazine. The window blinds are drawn but the sun is up. I'm wearing fleece but it's not cold outside.

If I'm thirty, then our daughter is six. She's the star of the show. Her box of blocks comes up to her shoulders. When the blocks are assembled, they'll build a whole airport, passenger plane and working luggage carousel included. Our daughter is wearing an oversized white T-shirt with her plaid bottoms. Her thin arms are pale. She's standing in front of my wife's cedar chest. A sixteen-inch TV, as deep as it is wide, sits atop the cedar chest, and a potted poinsettia sits atop the TV. Our daughter is looking down at the box. Her long brown hair curtains her face. She's angling the box to show her brother. With a proprietary air, she's explaining what it is.

Her little brother is crouched in front of her, back to the camera. He's two. He's sitting on his haunches, arms wrapped around his knees, balancing on his heels. His hair is fine, and his head is too big for his body. His ears are perfect. He's wearing a gray pullover. He's clearly riveted by his sister's explanation. I can't see his face, but I know he's smiling.

I'm most interested, though, in the action at the photo's far right. There's a small pop-up tent patterned like an igloo. A grown man could, if pressed, almost fit inside. A pile of books has already been loaded into this igloo. The baby is exiting the tent. He's nine months old. His plaid bottoms extend a good four inches past the ends of his feet. His wispy hair is almost blond. But the baby is not aiming at the box of blocks. He's not interested in what his brother and sister are doing. His attention is fixed on the half-read book his sister has just set aside. The book is splayed open, face down on the floor, saving her page. The baby has got the book by the spine. He's reading it upside down.

The baby's brother and sister are striking a pose for the camera, they're playing along for posterity. But the baby couldn't care less about all that. He radiates focus and intensity. He beelines for the book as soon as his sister puts it down, his curiosity palpable. For now, for him, there is nothing in the world but this book.

In a moment, after the photo has been taken, we'll notice what he's got. And then we'll rescue the paperback from his damp grip. And then he'll cry. He'll cry for the loss of an upside-down book he cannot read. He'll cry for—he knows not what.

When the book is taken, why does the baby cry?

What does he lose? A book?

Nothing so much as the severed intensity of the connection itself. Nothing so much as the awe he felt grasping after the marvel of it.

"Stand in awe," the Psalmist commands, "and be still" (Psalm 4:4). Or, again: "Let all the earth fear the Lord: let all the inhabitants of the world stand in awe of him" (Psalm 33:8).

When was the last time I stood in awe of anything? When was the last time I feared and worshipped the marvel that is my God? When was the last time I showed enough wisdom to greet the world with joy like a child?

Of the four New Testament Gospels, only Matthew talks about wise men.

Luke is focused on Mary and the shepherds. Mark omits the nativity altogether, starting instead with Jesus's baptism. And while John waxes cosmic for a few poetic verses, he also basically starts with Jesus and the Baptist.

Matthew goes his own way.

Matthew 1 sketches Joseph's genealogy and then tells how

an angel appeared to Joseph in a dream. The angel promises Joseph that Mary will "bring forth a son" and that this child will "save his people from their sins" (Matthew 1:21). After recounting this angelic visit, Matthew tersely covers a hundred verses of Lukan content with just one line: so Mary "brought forth her firstborn son" and they "called his name Jesus" (Matthew 1:25).

Matthew 2, then, skips directly—and uniquely—to the story of the wise men.

The wise men come from "the east" and ask Herod: "Where is he that is born King of the Jews? for we have seen his star in the east, and are come to worship him" (Matthew 2:1–2). Herod is troubled by this question, consults his priests and scribes, points the wise men toward Bethlehem, and asks to be informed when the new king is found. Freshly oriented, the wise men continue to follow their star "till it came and stood over where the young child was" and "they rejoiced with exceeding great joy" (Matthew 2:9–10). Upon entering "the house" in Bethlehem marked by the star, "they saw the young child with Mary his mother, and fell down, and worshipped him: and when they had opened their treasures, they presented unto him gifts; gold, and frankincense, and myrrh" (Matthew 2:11). Then, warned by God in a dream "that they should not return to Herod, they departed into their own country another way" (Matthew 2:12).

That's the sum total of what we know about the wise

men. Everything else is supposition, tradition, and popular imagination.

For the sake of simplicity, our own Christmas nativities set figurines of Matthew's wise men side by side with Luke's shepherds at Jesus's manger. But Luke never mentions wise men and Matthew never mentions shepherds, inns, or mangers. In fact, rather than visiting a newborn baby, Matthew's wise men visit a "young child." And rather than simply passing through Bethlehem, Jesus and his family appear to be living there in a "house" (Matthew 2:11).

How many wise men were there? Matthew doesn't say. More than one. Our best guess, traditionally, is that there were three—because, after all, they gave three gifts.

Where did the wise men come from? Matthew doesn't say. All we know is that these men came, mysteriously, from "the east," implying they were Gentiles, not Israelites.

What is a "wise man" exactly? Again, Matthew doesn't say. In Greek, the word Matthew uses is *magoi*. The wise men are—as we still say today—magi, a word associated with priestly experts in magic, astrology, and the interpretation of dreams. Matthew's wise men don't, in these verses, perform any wonders, but they do have ready access to royalty (see Matthew 2:1), they do possess wealth (see Matthew 2:11), they are keenly interested in stars (see Matthew 2:2, 9), and they are guided by dreams (see Matthew 2:12). With respect to being "magi," they fit the bill.

In our family, I've always insisted on referring—with a wink—to Matthew's wise men as "the three philosophers."

"Of course," I say, "the philosophers were there at the start. Who else? Just sheep and shepherds?"

This reading has yet to catch on.

When Matthew compresses a hundred verses of Luke's nativity into just one line, what does he omit? Essentially, he omits Mary. He omits the mother of the Son of God.

He omits the Annunciation—Gabriel's angelic announcement to Mary (see Luke 1:26–37). He omits Mary's faithful response: "Behold the handmaid of the Lord; be it unto me according to thy word" (Luke 1:38). He omits Mary's visit with Elisabeth (see Luke 1:39–56). And, especially, he omits what's called the Magnificat, the "song of Mary," that expresses Mary's own—and unmatched—expression of awe at the fact of the child growing within her:

My soul doth magnify the Lord,
And my spirit hath rejoiced in God my Saviour.
For he hath regarded the low estate of his handmaiden:
For, behold, from henceforth all generations shall call me blessed.

For he that is mighty hath done to me great things;
And holy is his name.
And his mercy is on them that fear him from generation to generation.
He hath shewed strength with his arm;
He hath scattered the proud in the imagination of their hearts.
He hath put down the mighty from their seats,
And exalted them of low degree.
He hath filled the hungry with good things;
And the rich he hath sent empty away.
He hath holpen his servant Israel, in remembrance of his mercy;
As he spake to our fathers, to Abraham, and to his seed for ever.[1]

Regardless of all he leaves unsaid about Mary and Elisabeth and the shepherds, Matthew does say what matters most about the wise men. Unmistakably, Matthew's wise men are bent on doing just one thing: they want to *worship*.

"We have seen his star in the east," they tell Herod, "and are come to worship him" (Matthew 2:2). And then, when they finally find the child, "they rejoiced with exceeding great joy" and "fell down, and worshipped him" (Matthew 2:10, 11).

In broad strokes, the magi have long been understood

to represent the knowledge and power of the Gentile world. But this investment of authority doesn't stop them from worshipping a child. And in worshipping this child, they appear to find what Mary found: they find themselves magnified by awe and joy.

Worshipping this child, they share the mind of that child.

Kneeling before the Christ Child, they become "submissive, meek, humble, patient, full of love" (Mosiah 3:19).

Kneeling in awe, they're born again.

The world pours in through our senses. It pours in through sights, sounds, tastes, smells, and feelings. Minds manage this flow. They regulate and organize the flood of information. For children, this flow is robust and intense. But the minds of adults typically work like a reducing valve, squeezing this intense flow back to a familiar trickle.

Or we could say, the minds of children prioritize the work of building up neurological connections. The transition to an adult mind, however, turns on pruning these connections. Adult minds trim these connections back to strengthen and isolate just those few that seem to matter most for our own survival. And then, going forward, adult minds default to filtering the whole world through that narrow, defensive aperture.

This, obviously, has many natural advantages. But a spontaneous and childlike capacity for awe, creativity, and love doesn't tend to be among them.

This tendency of adult minds to harden into inflexible, defensive shapes that can't see past the habitual screen of their own repetitive, self-absorbed fixations—this is what our scriptures call "sin."

The mind of a baby, Gopnik suggests, is like a lantern. The mind of an adult is like a spotlight. Lanterns fill the whole room with light. Spotlights single out just one thing. As a result, "it's plausible that babies are actually aware of much more, much more intensely than we are. The attentional spotlight in adults seems more like an attentional lantern for babies. Instead of experiencing a single aspect of their world and shutting down everything else," babies "seem to be vividly experiencing everything at once."[2]

"Ye are the light of the world. A city that is set on an hill cannot be hid. Neither do men light a candle, and put it under a bushel, but on a candlestick; and it giveth light unto all that are in the house" (Matthew 5:14–15).

A child is a light on the hill that cannot be hid. A child's light fills the whole house.

This capacity for open and unfiltered receptivity is, Gopnik notes, what we traditionally call awe. "Awe: our sense of the richness and complexity of the universe outside our own immediate concerns. It's the experience of standing outside on a dark night and gazing up at the infinite multitude of stars." (Stars, again.) And Gopnik's argument is that "babies and young children experience this kind of feeling, this lantern consciousness, all the time."[3]

Rather than filtering the world through just our own immediate concerns, awe opens the mind's aperture wide. Rather than prescreening what's seen, awe is about seeing whatever is given. Awe is about receiving, not selecting. "Rather than determining what to look at in the world, babies seem to let the world determine what they look at." As a result, babies "aren't just picking up information about the specific objects that are useful to them—they are picking up information about all the objects around them, especially when that information is new."[4]

Awe, like love, is often difficult and inconvenient. It's intense and overwhelming. It requires sacrifice and submission. Because awe overwhelms, it asks us to trust and yield control. It asks us to let God prevail. This is the price of admission.

"Of such is the kingdom of God" and "whosoever shall not receive the kingdom of God as a little child, he shall not enter therein" (Mark 10:14–15).

There is no other door.

If you think you can find God without living in awe—without worship—good luck.

Filled with awe, the whole world—including you—is born again. Everything is seen (again) for the first time. Everything is new.

With tender hearts and wide-open minds, babies are attuned to anything new and unexpected. "Presenting something that is even subtly unexpected immediately rivets a baby's attention and they will reliably look at unexpected events for longer than expected ones. Babies seem to have an infinitely voracious appetite for the unexpected."[5]

It follows, then, that doing things like traveling or learning a new skill can help us feel like children again. Traveling, the grip of habit loosens and we're forced outside ourselves. Everything foreign is vivid. Everything unassimilated shines. Even ordinary things—door handles, electric sockets, coins—draw attention and subvert routine. Traveling, we're like children again. We stumble. We're awkward. We don't quite know what to do. We're "vividly aware of everything without being focused on any one thing in particular."[6]

Or, similarly, "when we first master a new skill, such as riding a bike or using a new computer program, we are painfully conscious of every step. But by the time we become expert we can literally be completely unconscious of what we are doing" and whole days can pass—whole lives can pass—on autopilot, as we live like "perfectly functional, walking, talking, teaching, meeting-attending zombies."[7]

Shunryu Suzuki called the child's open and ready mind "beginner's mind." Or even more simply, "big mind."[8] To be converted is to recover, as an adult, the willing intensity of this big mind.

The mind of Christ is a beginner's mind. His mind is always starting over. "For I will be merciful," he promises, "and their sins and their iniquities will I remember no more" (Hebrews 8:12).

Always ready to begin again, Christ's mind is the biggest mind.

Worshipping the Christ Child, attuned to any new sign in the heavens, Matthew's wise men also have big minds. In the traditional Christian calendar, their arrival in Bethlehem is celebrated on January 6. Richard Trexler notes in his excellent study of the magi that for almost two thousand years, "the faithful in most of western Europe have thought that these wise men arrived at the crib on that same date, the twelfth day of Christmas, when Jesus was thirteen days old." Often, this celebration also coincided with "the feast of the kings, when Balthazar, Melchior, and Caspar"—as the Western Christian tradition creatively named the magi—"had their annual moment in the sun."[9]

These twelve days—between December 25 and January 6—are the "twelve days of Christmas."

My father loved Christmas. He was always looking for ways to stretch out the holiday. When I was eight or nine, he started a new tradition in our family called "the twelve days of Christmas." He would wrap twelve presents and number them. Rather than placing them under the tree, he would arrange these twelve on our rough stone fireplace. Then starting on December 13, he would gather us around each night and have us guess which presents were meant for us. Whoever guessed right got to open their present early.

My father, though, had a notoriously hard time remembering which presents were actually meant for whom. He kept these presents not only a secret from my mother but, often enough, himself. This was half the fun. Even carrying a numbered list in his overstuffed wallet didn't solve the problem.

I only learned later that—of course?—my father was doing the twelve days of Christmas backwards. The twelve days don't come *before* Christmas, they come *after*. Mercifully, such details never gave my father pause.

Traditional celebrations of the magi's arrival on January 6 are called "the feast of Jesus' 'epiphany,'" with *epiphany* being "a word that means 'appearance' or 'manifestation,' 'revelation' or 'coming out.'"[10]

Epiphany: the surprising appearance of a divine being, the

sudden manifestation of an essential meaning, an intuitive grasp of reality triggered by a simple and striking event.

What better way to celebrate Christmas than with a feast of epiphanies? And what better way to describe the awe-filled mind of a child than as—in itself—a feast of epiphanies?

Am I hungry? When was my last epiphany? When was my last feast of epiphanies? When did I last step outside with a bare head on a cold January night, unafraid of the dark, to fix my eyes unblinking on the circling stars?

Don't I spend my days doing just the opposite?

As an adult, don't I spend my days hiding from epiphany?

Watch me: I'm old. I spend my days with all the cupboards stocked and all the lights burning and all the screens streaming. I spend my days with all the doors locked against epiphany.

Awe might knock, but who would dare answer?

Awe, like love, is difficult and inconvenient. It's intense and overwhelming. It requires sacrifice and submission.

In the imagination of some early Christians, the new star seen by the wise men was sometimes, quite intentionally, conflated with Emperor Constantine's own famous heavenly vision. Before Constantine, Christian art commonly represented the magi's star as "six-pointed," but Constantine's own "vision of a heavenly object, though it was not called a star in the sources, reshaped what the magi saw."[11]

What did Constantine, Rome's first "Christian" emperor, claim to see in the heavens that fateful day when the empire itself pivoted toward Christianity? He claimed to see the first two letters of Christ's name—in Greek, *chi* (X) and *rho* (P)—superimposed in a shape suggesting Christ's own cross.

Imagine the wise men following *this* astral sign through the night, the blazing sign of Christ's cross, as it guides them to the child. Imagine them kneeling beneath it, surrendering their gifts and worshipping with awe and joy. Imagine them being reborn beneath the sign of the cross.

If I've barricaded the doors against love and awe, this is surely why: because, to be reborn, I must first be willing to die. To worship the Christ Child, I must follow the cross. I must be baptized in both water and fire. I must die and be buried and be born again.

"Know ye not," Paul asks, "that so many of us as were baptized into Jesus Christ were baptized into his death? Therefore we are buried with him by baptism into death: that like as Christ was raised up from the dead by the glory of the Father, even so we also should walk in newness of life" (Romans 6:3–4).

This is Christmas: birth, death, rebirth. Though grown, I'm a child again. Though dying, I'm still being born. "I am crucified with Christ: nevertheless I live" (Galatians 2:20).

Filled with awe, I have an epiphany. I have *the* epiphany. I start seeing what was unseen. I start hearing what was unheard. I start feeling what was unfelt.

Filled with awe, my mind opens wide, single to the glory of God, undefended, flooded with light.

My mind is Christ's mind.

And once I share this mind, "Christ liveth in me" (Galatians 2:20).

CHAPTER TWO

Imagination

In the photo, I'm a father. It's Christmas Eve.

This time, though, the photographer is me. Technically, I'm behind rather than in the photo. I'm present as the photo's point of view. And that point of view does feel familiar: the height, the angle, the posture. These are my own. Everyone else in the photo is arranged in a classic Christmas tableau: three angels declare glad tidings to two shepherds and a dog. My wife, daughter, and son play the angels. My wife's mom and dad play the shepherds. The dog is the dog.

The photo was printed in January 2006, so it's Christmas 2005.

Impossibly, I'm not even thirty.

We're in Las Vegas, visiting my in-laws for Christmas. The house is on the edge of the city, up against the mountains. Everything is desert scrub, gated communities, and concrete washes. A sea of neon lights blinks in the distance. We're in the living room. The walls are white and the carpet is brown. The house is newly built. An empty nest. The sun is down but the weather is mild.

My wife, an angel, is standing with one hand upraised, waving a wand tipped with a bright pink star. Her hair is short and brown, wreathed by a plastic tiara. She's wearing a loose denim jumper. Red flowers ring the hem. To play her part, she also has a short satin jacket, golden, borrowed from a childhood box of dress-up clothes. She's smiling—but her eyebrows are cocked like she wants me to please take this picture already. The swell of her denim jumper shows she's expecting. In about eleven weeks, the baby will be born. The doctors warn he may need to come early. On the wall behind my wife, there's a family photo. Though only one is visible here, that living room wall displays thirty family photos, one a year for thirty years, arranged chronologically. These photos are like tree rings—time itself cross-sectioned and framed.

My wife is holding a toddler on her hip. This boy is fifteen months old, a big baby with rolls of fat. His cheeks are round. He's got a pacifier. Though he's wearing black sweats, an orange shirt, and Winnie the Pooh slippers, he's also clearly an angel. Like his mother, he's adorned with a plastic halo. And in place of a golden coat, he's got an angel's vest, black felt with red piping, borrowed from the same dress-up box. He's not looking at the camera. As always, his attention is fixed on his sister.

His sister is centered again. She's also holding a star-tipped wand, waving it above her head. She's full of great joy. Her hair is tucked behind her ears but loose across her shoulders. She's five. Already dressed in white pajamas, she doesn't need any additional costuming. She's looking straight at the camera. A trace of red-eye from the flash. For additional height, she's standing on a child-sized rocking chair made for her mom. It's positioned in front of the TV. A pair of TV antennas, augmented with loose sheets of tin foil, hover over the whole scene.

Both shepherds are wearing the requisite bathrobes and headbands. One bathrobe is blue, the other is red with penguins. The shepherds are kneeling, drawing attention to the height from which the angels have descended. Grandpa is leaning on his shepherd's staff, facing me. Grandma is turned away. With one hand, she's shielding her eyes from all that angelic light. With the other, she's petting the dog, holding him to his mark. The dog is something like a black lab. A red bandana is tied over his collar to show he's with the shepherds. He, too, is looking away, his ears flattened against his head, a touch embarrassed. The shepherds kneel in front of a short bookcase. An empty red stocking hangs from one shelf. A pair of little ladies, crocheted from thick yarn and shaped like bells—one red, one green—are perched on top of the bookcase. They have real bells inside and jingle when you ring them.

Everyone is smiling. Everyone is playing.

Everyone is imagining they were there when God was born.

This power to imagine—to play and create and envision new worlds—is characteristic of a child's mind. And, too, this power is vital to life itself. Without this power to imagine new futures and other worlds, life contracts to a black nub. Absent possibility, reality collapses into blunt actuality. Hope decays. Light gives way to darkness. Life cedes to death.

"Where there is no vision, the people perish" (Proverbs 29:18).

While John is silent about Christ's birth, his Gospel does open with a poem praising God's power to imagine new worlds. In place of narrating Christ's nativity, John sings a cosmic hymn about how the world itself was born, invoking God as Creator and Christ as Word.

"In the beginning," John says, "was the Word, and the Word was with God, and the Word was God. The same was in the beginning with God. All things were made by him; and without him was not any thing made that was made" (John 1:1–3).

In our King James English, John calls Christ "the Word." This is good. But in Greek, the word John uses is *logos*. This is better.

Logos is an ordinary word, but dense with meaning. It means word or saying. It means doctrine, teaching, or maxim. But logos also means reason, as in "logic." It means cause, explanation, or plan. To name Christ as the Word who created all things is to name Christ as the Mind or Reason at the root of all things. It's to speak of Christ as the originating plan, the founding template, the governing blueprint for all the creative work that follows.

In the beginning, John says, the Mind of God imagined a new world.

And this Mind was with God.

And this Mind was God.

All things were made by this Mind and without this Mind nothing was made.

In this Mind "was life; and the life was the light of men. And the light shineth in darkness; and the darkness comprehended it not" (John 1:4–5).

This is the mind of Christ, the mind of a child: a place of great power and possibility, where new worlds are continually imagined and blueprints for these new worlds are endlessly unfurled.

The mind of Christ is a womb and the world itself is his child.

Imagine Jesus as a child. He's two or three. He's digging in the dirt as Mary watches from the door. He's smoothing roads with a scrap of wood. He's wetting clay into blocks for houses. He digs a little well. He mounds a hill outside the city walls and plants three sticks as trees. He hollows out a cave. He imagines the streets of his town thronged with multitudes. These multitudes are looking for God. He's playing make-believe.

Is this what the Son of God was doing when the wise men finally arrived? Was he playing in the dirt?

And if so, is this what the wise men imagined they would find? Is this what they traveled all that way to see?

The wise men, at least to start, seem to have been looking for something more conventional. Searching for the child, their first guess was to stop at a palace and ask for directions.

But the wise men proved adaptable, their minds flexible, their imaginations strong. All that daily work of staring into the heavens, of filling their eyes again and again with stars, must have worked to keep their minds open and plastic, their hearts soft and pliable.

When they do finally find him, the wise men don't hesitate to worship. Surprised as they may have been, they don't hesitate to offer their gifts. They don't hesitate to cast their lots with this new kingdom they have—only now and with God's help—begun to see.

"Blessed are your eyes," Jesus says, "for they see: and your ears, for they hear" (Matthew 13:16).

"There has been a great difficulty in getting anything into the heads of this generation," Joseph Smith lamented in 1843. "It has been like splitting hemlock knots with a corn dodger for a wedge, and a pumpkin for a beetle. Even the Saints are slow to understand. I have tried for a number of years to get the minds of the saints prepared to receive the things of God, but we frequently see some of them, after suffering all they have for the work of God will fly to pieces like glass, as soon as anything comes that is contrary to their traditions; they cannot stand the fire at all; how many will be able to abide a celestial law and go through, and receive their exaltation, I am unable to say."[1]

This, though, *is* what children can do. Children can bend rather than break. They can stand the fire. They can embrace the unexpected. They can imagine something new.

Children not only see more of what's actual, they imagine more of what's possible.

"As soon as babies can talk," Alison Gopnik finds, "they immediately talk about the possible as well as the real."[2] By imagining, pretending, and playing, "young children explore the magic of human possibility in a particularly wide-ranging and creative way"; they "move into the world of the possible with particular ease."[3] In this way, as Gopnik puts it, "children are the R&D department of the human species—the blue-sky guys, the brainstormers."[4] Children don't "explore only the possibilities that might be useful—they explore all the possibilities."[5]

Recall that a child's mind is more like a lantern than a spotlight. Picture, then, a lantern bright enough to show not only the truth about this present world, but also the truth about all those future worlds that, to us, seem impossible.

How strong is God's imagination? How big is God's mind? How many possibilities can it compass?

This is the question the angel must answer when Mary herself asks how it's possible for her, a virgin, and Elisabeth, "well stricken in years," to bear their promised children: "With God," Gabriel attests, "nothing shall be impossible" (Luke 1:18, 37).

This, too, is a good test for assessing conversion, for

measuring how much like a child I am: can I imagine the kingdom of God? Can I see it in my mind's eye?

Jesus told Nicodemus that before a man can "enter into the kingdom of God," he must first become a child even to *see* it (John 3:5). "Except a man be born again," Jesus stressed, "he cannot see the kingdom of God" (John 3:3).

Can I see the kingdom of God?

Can I, like a child, imagine a new world? A different world? A better world?

Can I imagine a "better" world that amounts to anything more than the repetitive satisfaction of my most predictable desires?

How would my new world be, in any way, genuinely new? How would it surprise me, defy me, bring me to tears, cause me to marvel, fill me with awe, empower me to love?

How, exactly, might my new world be an epiphany?

Are my graying powers of imagination good for anything more than vanity and fear?

What if my eternal salvation depended on imagining a new world? What if Jesus met me at the pearly gates, embraced me, and told me I was welcome in heaven—I just needed, first, to show him I could imagine something new? Even just one, small, genuinely new thing?

Could I do it? Could I prove that my mind is, in any way, like the mind of a child?

Could I prove that my mind is, in any way, like his?

The book of Ecclesiastes is narrated by a Solomonic figure whose imagination has run dry. He has sampled every pleasure, amassed every prize, achieved every goal. "I was great," this great man says, "and increased more than all that were before me" (Ecclesiastes 2:9).

But now he's old—especially in mind—and, to him, everything seems vain. "Vanity of vanities," he repeats, "vanity of vanities; all is vanity" (Ecclesiastes 1:2).

Why has everything become vain?

Because, the old man confesses, he can't see anything new.

"There is nothing new under the sun" (Ecclesiastes 1:9, NIV).

Most of what we traditionally say about the wise men is pure invention: how many they were, whether they had one homeland or several, whether they came from Africa, Persia, or India, whether they were priests or kings, whether they were young or old—even whether they were, as some have suggested, philosophers. But Matthew's skeletal descriptions, teasing and indirect as they are, invite us to play with these outlines and fill in the gaps.

Christians have never been shy about filling in these gaps. From the start, they scoured the Hebrew Bible for raw materials, for prophetic clues about how to imagine the magi. They found any number of passages that seemed to put flesh on Matthew's bones.

Psalm 72:10–11 seemed like an obvious parallel: "The kings of Tarshish and of the isles shall bring presents: the kings of Sheba and Seba shall offer gifts. Yea, all kings shall fall down before him: all nations shall serve him."

And from all of Isaiah's prophecies, Isaiah 60 was an early favorite:

> *Nations come to your light,*
> *kings to your bright light.*
> *Look all around you!*
> *They all gather and come to you—*
> . . .
> *For the riches of distant lands will belong to you,*
> *and the wealth of nations will come to you.*
> *Camel caravans will cover your roads,*
> *young camels from Midian and Ephah.*
> *All the merchants of Sheba will come,*
> *bringing gold and incense*
> *and singing praises to the Lord.*
> *(Isaiah 60:3–6, New English Translation)*

You know these songs of praise. This is still how we, with

the wise men, sing to the Lord: "Star of wonder, star of night, / Star with royal beauty bright, / Westward leading, / Still proceeding, / Guide us to Thy perfect Light."[6]

Christians have also never been shy about repurposing extant festivals as Christian holy days. In both Eastern and Western traditions, Christians gladly combined celebrations of the magi with "the ancient practice of electing and crowning seasonal or festive kings."[7] In this way, Matthew's three "magi" were reimagined as three "kings" and, given the festival framework, people naturally began to act out the parts, recreating the magi's visit to the Christ Child on the twelfth day of Christmas.

"We three kings of Orient are, / Bearing gifts we traverse afar, / Field and fountain, / Moor and mountain, / Following yonder star."[8]

These seasonal festivals, recycled for Epiphany, were public spectacles and often involved full-scale parades through the city streets. In early versions of the celebration, the collective procession ended "at 'the crib,' which, before taking on its modern shape, was just the main altar of the church" where wooden statues of Mary and Jesus waited to receive their gifts.[9] From roughly AD 1200 to 1500, kings and rulers "presented *themselves* in the guise of the magi to great outdoor urban audiences."[10] Still later traditions had children and beggars imagine they were the magi, using the celebration as an occasion for the poor to collect charitable "gifts" on behalf of the Christ Child.[11]

Static crèches, as opposed to mobile processions, can be dated from the late thirteenth and early fourteenth centuries. "They were commonly but not necessarily located in a church chapel, but they might also be found at the entrance to a church, near the town hall or, somewhat later, in people's homes. From early on, they consisted either of a simple nativity scene—with a minimum of three separate figures—or of a more complicated adoration scene."[12] The ascendence of crèches, though, didn't dissuade people from inserting themselves into the drama as shepherds or wise men. "The structure of the crèche," Richard Trexler reports, still "encouraged devotees to take their place in it."[13]

For thousands of years now, we've been pretending to be wise men. We've assigned the parts, dressed up in costumes, and acted out the stories. We've imagined we were shepherds and kings.

As a child, I don't remember ever displaying a crèche in our yard or staging a pageant in our living room. Not so for my wife. Or, then, for our own children. For them, Christmas pageants were a fixture of the season.

These days, on Christmas Eve, we bake a birthday cake for Jesus. Always an angel food cake that, to keep from collapsing, must cool upside down. We frost it with whipped cream. We light candles, sing happy birthday, and blow them out.

Happy birthday, Jesus.

"When our children were little," President Henry B. Eyring recalled, "we created a family Christmas pageant." Early versions of the Eyring family pageant only called for three players: Joseph, Mary, and Jesus. But as their family grew, the cast also grew to include "kings bearing jeweled boxes to honor the newborn King." The Eyrings also added a prologue centered on Samuel the Lamanite, including "a disbelieving crowd armed with aluminum foil balls to throw at Samuel" as he stood atop the city wall. This scene, though, eventually became problematic. As their children got bigger, President Eyring lamented, and "members of the angry mob grew stronger and more accurate, we had to remind them forcefully that Samuel could *not* be hit because he was God's protected servant—and because we were inviting and celebrating peace!"[14]

This, though, is what children do. They can hardly help themselves. They invent, they embroider, they improvise. It's hard for them to stick to the script. They keep finding—naturally, spontaneously—new variations on old themes. They keep exploring. They keep imagining.

Hand a child a snow globe. They will flip it over and shake it hard. They will use both hands. They will use their arms, shoulders, hips, and knees. They will jump and spin.

Children can't help but turn the world upside down.

In Old Testament Hebrew, the word for repentance is *teshuva*. The root meaning of this word is to "turn" or "return." To repent, I must turn back toward God. I must return to the beginning. I must start over. I must turn life on its head and set it aswirl. I must be born again.

In New Testament Greek, the word for repentance is *metanoia*, as when Jesus says, "The time is fulfilled, and the kingdom of God is at hand: repent ye [*metanoeite*], and believe the gospel" (Mark 1:15). In Greek, *nous* is the word for "mind" and so, the root meaning of *metanoia* isn't to "turn" but simply "to change one's mind," or even just "to think differently."

To repent is to think differently.

The time has come, Jesus says, to repent, to think differently, to reason like a child, to have even a little imagination, to give up your tired ways, to finally believe my good news, to see how the kingdom of God is already right here, right in front of you, staring you right in the eye.

To repent: to change my mind for Christ's.

It's useful for children to do what grown-ups call "play." It's helpful for them to explore what Gopnik calls the realm of "counterfactuals," that halo of possible worlds that wreaths the hard facts of our own.

This impulse to imagine, to engage in "obsessive and unstoppable pretend play," Gopnik argues, "reflects the most sophisticated, important, and characteristic human abilities."[15] This impulse is especially crucial because this "ability to imagine possible worlds is closely tied to our ability to think causally," that is, to our ability to think in terms of causes and effects, and, thus, to our ability to discern the sometimes ambiguous—but always vital—connections between actions and consequences.[16]

To play is to explore. When children play, they're conducting thought experiments. They're running simulations that allow them to test, with minimal cost and risk, what's load-bearing in this world and what isn't. When children play, they're gathering data, funneling variables, and isolating causal mechanisms.

What is this world? What can it be?

What am I? What can I be?

These playful experiments help children to map their world—and, then, to extend these maps into blueprints for what may yet be possible.

Every true act of repentance is, at least in part, a childlike act of imagination.

Christ's atonement is an engine for coining fresh counterfactuals.

Life contracts to a black nub. Our possible futures collapse into blunt inevitability.

Christ pushes back against this collapse. He stretches his arms wide as eternity, shoulders the weight of inevitable consequences, and makes space for something new.

As a sinner, I'm locked inside what's actual. I'm condemned to be only what I am. My mind is a broken record, skipping every time life's needle hits that jagged scratch.

Repeat. Repeat. Repeat.

Vanity. Vanity. Vanity.

There's nothing new under the sun.

A slave to sin, nothing new is possible.

Christ saves us from this vanity. His mind is the biggest and his imagination is the strongest. He's the universe's leading expert in counterfactuals. He sees all of what's actual and the whole of what's possible. He sees not only what things are but what they may still be.

Christ creates. He invents. He re-creates.

Christ speaks and entire worlds leap into being.

He calls out and the blind see, the lame walk, the dead rise.

He forgives and everything is forgiven, everything is new, everything begins again.

"And suddenly there was with the angel a multitude of the heavenly host praising God, and saying, Glory to God in the highest, and on earth peace, good will toward men" (Luke 2:13–14).

This is Christmas.

Christ hands me a snow globe and I shake it hard.

I repent. I turn around. I join him. I change my mind. I'm a child again.

I can play and explore and pretend. I can see how things could be different. I can see the kingdom of God.

I can join Christ in imagining how *I* could be different.

Remade, I imagine I'm a wise man. I imagine I'm a shepherd. I imagine I'm a philosopher-king. I put on my blue bathrobe and, fixing my eyes on the horizon, cinch the robe's fuzzy sash around my forehead. I shield my eyes from all that angelic light. I hush my camel. I hold the dog to his mark. My pockets are full of foil balls.

I imagine I was there at the beginning when Christ was born.

And, too, I imagine Christ is there to meet me at the end.

I imagine meeting him at heaven's gates. I imagine returning his embrace and showing him something surprising, something entirely new.

I show him something I never could have guessed.

I show him me.

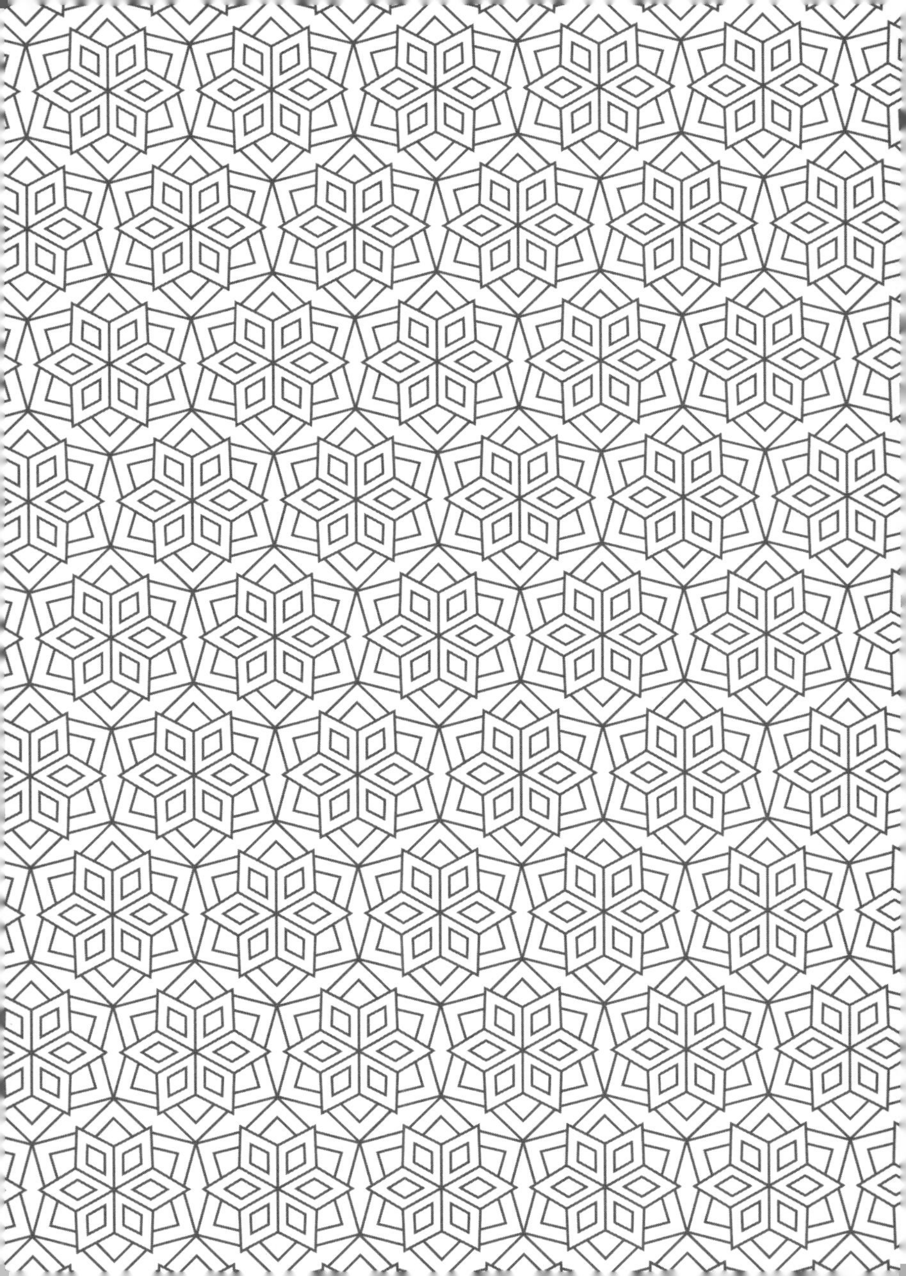

CHAPTER THREE

Love

In the photo, I'm a husband. Barely. It's almost Christmas.

There are ten people in the photo, arranged in two rows. My wife is centered. She's flanked by our mothers. Her little brother is kneeling. The back row consists of two fathers, three bridesmaids, and myself, all standing. I'm wearing a black tuxedo, a black vest, a black bow tie, and a white shirt with a wing collar and black pearl buttons. All of this is rented. My boutonniere consists of one white rose pinned, for some reason, to my right lapel. In every other photo, it's pinned to my left. My glasses are round with wire frames. They catch the light. My hair is, for me, relatively long. You would call it short. I'm standing immediately behind the bride, arms loose at my sides. I'm tall. I'm clean-shaven. I'm smiling like I'm in love.

There's no date on the photo. It's December 22, 1998.

I'm twenty-two years old.

The photo was taken at our wedding reception in Las Vegas. We're in the cultural hall of my wife's hometown chapel. Basketball lines are visible on the hardwood floor. A bridesmaid has one foot out of bounds. Everything is cranberry and gold, Christmas-tinged, and intensely Mormon. The lighting is dim. The group is backed by a white trellis, trifold, draped in sheer white fabric and decked with pine boughs, pinecones, and white Christmas lights. A traditional Christmas wreath with poinsettias and a gold bow hangs in the center. Night has fallen. A desert wind is blowing.

The bridesmaids are all wearing identical dresses—gold, short-sleeved, floor-length, empire waists. Two are friends of the bride, one is the bride's sister. Of the friends, one is her best friend from high school and the other is her best friend from college. Her best friend from college is, now, one of my best friends. We talked on the phone while I was writing this. Both friends are tall, both are pale with long dark hair, and both are smiling. Only one has bangs.

These bridesmaids stand next to me. The bride's younger sister, with her little brother, is off to the right. The sister, one can see, has already been asked to smile in many, many family photos today. The brother is wearing a dark suit and white shirt. As is pro forma for deacons, the shirt's collar is two sizes too big. He'll grow into it. To his credit, he's still making the face all children make when asked to smile on command: lips thin, teeth bared, eyes wild, eyebrows comically arched.

The mothers are seated on either side of the bride, angled inward, hands in their laps. They're both wearing cranberry skirts and matching jackets. These outfits are similar but not identical. Their expressions, too, are similar but not identical. The difference, I think, is largely a measure of how much practice they've had. This is my mother-in-law's first chance to stage a wedding. She looks happy but a little overwhelmed, like her heart and mind, after months of planning, are still racing to catch up with the day. Not so for my mother. This is her third time. Her eyes are sparkling. She looks relaxed and immensely pleased—like someone who's just won an unexpected prize, like a cat who's swallowed a canary, like she can't quite believe I've pulled this off.

The fathers, paternal, anchor the back row. Like the brother, they're both wearing dark suits and white shirts, not tuxedos. My father-in-law's tie is, as requested, solid cranberry. He seems both cheerful and amused. My own father's tie is not cranberry. It does have a splash of muted red—dusty rose?—but it's mostly blues and grays. Like my mother, he seems quite relaxed. His shoulders are broad and his stomach round. He's the only one with his hands in his pockets. His smile is soft and his eyes narrowed, as if, moments before the photo was taken, he'd just been nodding in agreement with a well-pitched plan.

This is the core of the wedding party. Parents, siblings, bridesmaids, groom.

What remains?

The bride.

The bride is radiant in white.

All the light in the photo bends toward her.

I love her.

Like Christ, children are quick to love, quick to trust, quick to forgive, quick to embrace.

They're built for empathy.

They feel what others feel.

They cry when we cry. They smile when we smile. They laugh when we laugh.

All their windows are open and all their doors unlocked.

This is atonement: in the garden and on the cross, Christ feels everything we feel.

"And he will take upon him death, that he may loose the bands of death which bind his people; and he will take upon him their infirmities, that his bowels may be filled with mercy, according to the flesh, that he may know according to the flesh how to succor his people" (Alma 7:12).

The Christmas story is, in many ways, a love story. And a

wedding story. And, thus, a nativity story—the story of a birth.

Matthew's opening move, first chapter, first verse, before even hinting about the wise men, is to declare "the genealogy of Jesus Christ, the son of David" (Matthew 1:1, NET). To this end, he unspools a long string of "begats," stretching all the way from Abraham to "Joseph the husband of Mary, of whom was born Jesus, who is called Christ" (Matthew 1:16).

In short, Matthew opens Jesus's story by listing nearly fifty babies.

This is good advice if you ever need to write a Gospel, if you're ever tasked with explaining God: pack the opening pages with as many babies as possible.

Biblical "begats" are love in its most concentrated narrative form.

Men, of course, don't "beget" babies themselves. Where, then, are all the mothers in these genealogies?

Both Matthew and Luke give genealogies for Jesus. But these genealogies—both curious—don't match (see Matthew 1:1–16 and Luke 3:23–38). It's been suggested that Matthew traces Joseph's line while Luke traces Mary's. But Joseph is not Jesus's father. And while Matthew's list does include five surprising women—Tamar, Rahab, Ruth, Bathsheba, and Mary—Luke's official list doesn't even include Mary.

The drama of Matthew's first chapter, foregrounding Joseph as it does, turns on whether Joseph and Mary will actually get married. The complication, of course, is that while "Mary was engaged to Joseph, but before they came together, she was found to be pregnant through the Holy Spirit" (Matthew 1:18, NET).

Joseph, understandably, is taken aback. And too, he must have been crushed. All signs point to his love for Mary. So being "a righteous man, and because he did not want to disgrace her, he intended to divorce her privately" (Matthew 1:19, NET).

Cue the angel of mercy, dispatched in a dream.

The angel tells Joseph: "Do not be afraid to take Mary as your wife" (Matthew 1:20, NET). And so, just like that, Joseph isn't afraid anymore. Fear vanishes. Love wins. And then, as soon as Joseph was "raised from sleep," he "did as the angel of the Lord had bidden him, and took unto him his wife: and knew her not till she had brought forth her firstborn son: and he called his name Jesus" (Matthew 1:24–25).

This has always been part of God's plan. "Therefore shall a man leave his father and his mother, and shall cleave unto his wife: and they shall be one flesh" (Genesis 2:24).

The Book of Mormon doesn't show any interest in Joseph or Davidic lines, but it does keep circling back to Mary. An angel tells Benjamin that Jesus's "mother shall be called Mary" (Mosiah 3:8). The Spirit tells Alma that Jesus "shall be born of Mary" (Alma 7:10). And when Nephi is given an explanation of the tree of life, Mary takes center stage.

"Caught away in the Spirit of the Lord," Nephi is shown the tree of life, a tree which is beautiful and white and "precious above all" (1 Nephi 11:1, 9). When he asks for "the interpretation thereof," he's shown a virgin who is "exceedingly fair and white," even "a virgin, most beautiful and fair above all other virgins" (1 Nephi 11:11, 13, 15). The fruit of this mother's womb, he's told, will be "the Son of God" and, what's more, that beautiful, white tree itself embodies "the love of God, which sheddeth itself abroad in the hearts of the children of men" (1 Nephi 11:18, 22).

The tree of life represents the love of God.

But to understand this love, Nephi must first understand Mary.

"One flesh" is, ultimately, a good description of Joseph and Mary's connection as husband and wife.

But it's probably an even better description of Mary's own connection with the baby, of what she felt when "she brought forth her firstborn son, and wrapped him in swaddling clothes, and laid him in a manger" (Luke 2:7). In this same way, it's a good description of most every mother's connection with their baby. Until the child is born and the cord is cut, mother and child are literally one flesh.

However, perhaps best of all, "one flesh" may be an excellent description of what it's like simply to *be* a baby. It may be an excellent description in general of a baby's experience, not only of its mother, but of the world at large.

For babies, the membrane between mind and world—between subject and object, between "self" and "other"—is thin, elastic, porous. Here, rather than marking a sharp divide between inside and outside, the difference between mind and world shows up only as a shallow fold in a single continuous surface.

For babies, the whole world is their body.

Baby and world are one flesh.

"Neither pray I for these alone, but for them also which shall believe on me through their word; that they all may be one; as thou, Father, art in me, and I in thee, that they also may be one in us" (John 17:20–21).

Babies and children have weak egos. They have a weak sense of self, a weak sense of themselves as a separate and independent "I." They may kick and scream and cry, but this isn't because they're selfish. It's because they *lack* a strong sense of self. They lack the defensive bulwark provided by a strong ego. Lacking these walls, they stand exposed and vulnerable to the world as it continually pours in.

To experience the world like an adult, you need a strong ego. You need a strong sense of self. And to have a strong ego, you need a compelling story. You need a story about your "self" that, for better and worse, you can sell yourself.

An adult "self" is, at bottom, a story.

And, in particular, an adult "self" is a story that dependably does two things at once.

First, an adult "self" is a story that casts you as the star of your own life. It casts you—or better, miscasts you—as the hero of your own story.

And second, given your now starring role, an adult story empowers you to see everything as part of that same story. It empowers you to read everything that happens *to* you as also being *about* you. With its ready and reductive narrative frame, it empowers you to easily interpret everything as being about what you deserve, whether you're loved, and when you'll finally get what you want.

By the time you're an adult, this story has enormous pull. It draws everything into your ego's orbit. With it, you can gather everything that happens into a single plot. And with it, you can slot every event into a single superstitious timeline that, in short order, starts to feel inevitable—with each event leading inexorably to the next, with your past deciding, in one blow, the whole of your present and your future. And before you know it, your whole life is on rails. And there's no slowing down. And there's no switching tracks.

Your "self" is now running the show.

Narrative momentum will take it from here.

This adult "self" is life's original conspiracy theory.

This kind of ego is exactly what children are missing.

Children are missing this story. They're missing this well-developed sense of personal narrative that continually casts them as the star and, thus, falsely positions them as the center of the universe.

"Babies and young children don't yet have autobiographical memory and executive control," Alison Gopnik writes. "They don't experience their lives as a single timeline stretching back into the past and forward into the future. They don't send themselves backward and forward along this timeline as adults do, recapturing for a moment that past self who was the miserable loser or the happy lover, or anticipating despairs and joys of the future. And they don't feel immersed in a constant stream of thoughts and feelings. In fact, for babies and young children there doesn't seem to be the same kind of 'me' making these projections into the past and future."[1] Rather, just the opposite. "Children start to weave these memories into a continuous narrative—a narrative in which they are the hero, or at least the protagonist—only when they are older."[2]

In other words, Gopnik argues, children lack "a single 'inner autobiographer.'" They don't have "the same kind of inner observer." They don't have "a sense of self" tied to "a single timeline." They lack the fiction of "an überself who negotiates between current, past, and future selves, and ultimately hands down the orders."[3]

What would this feel like?

What would it feel like to experience the world the way a child does? To have only an elastic, porous, and decentered sense of self? To not have every experience immediately taken hostage by your stale story? To experience time not as an inevitable, two-dimensional chain of causes and effects, but as an open, three-dimensional constellation of affinities and possibilities?

Or simply: what if your story went quiet?

What if that internal monologue—that interminably judgmental voice-over, that worried and fearful mental chatter that fills your head day and night—finally shut up?

How deep, then, would the world's silence run?

How silent would that night be? How holy?

How full of epiphanies?

What would happen if your story went silent? You would sleep—like a baby—in heavenly peace.

Lit by this silence, the whole world is calm and bright. The whole world feels—again—like a grace.

It feels like a gift.

It feels like you and the world are "one flesh."

It feels like love.

"I in them, and thou in me, that they may be made perfect in one" (John 17:23).

When the wise men finally found Jesus, when they finally "saw the young child with Mary his mother," what did they do? (Matthew 2:11). Matthew says they "fell down, and worshipped him" (Matthew 2:11).

But what did their worship look like?

It looked like this: they "opened their treasures" and "they presented unto him gifts; gold, and frankincense, and myrrh" (Matthew 2:11).

If you find yourself again with the mind of a child, what do you do? You start seeing your treasures as gifts. Filled with awe, you start loving. You start "opening your treasures" and sharing them around, as if you had no proper "self" to which they belonged. You start giving out all your treasures as if they were gifts, as if everything you'd ever been given was a gift that God meant you, in turn, to give.

"I would that ye should remember," Benjamin taught, "and always retain in remembrance, the greatness of God, and your own nothingness" (Mosiah 4:11).

And if I remember my ego's nothingness? Then "ye shall always rejoice, and be filled with the love of God" (Mosiah 4:12).

And then what will happen? Then "ye yourselves will succor those that stand in need of your succor; ye will administer of your substance unto him that standeth in need; and ye will not suffer that the beggar putteth up his petition to you in vain" (Mosiah 4:16).

Why did the wise men give these *particular* gifts—gold, frankincense, and myrrh? Matthew doesn't say.

Gold is a precious metal. Frankincense is a fragrant gum. Myrrh is an aromatic spice.

Traditionally, these gifts were assigned specific symbolic roles. Gold, used for royal crowns, was associated with Christ's kingship. Frankincense, used for priestly incense, was associated with Christ's divinity. And myrrh, used for healing and embalming, was associated with Christ's humanity and mortality.

In one of my favorite stories about these treasures, the wise men use these gifts to test Jesus. "The wise men are said to have offered gold, frankincense, and myrrh," Richard Trexler recounts, "so as to determine just what the child's status was. They meant to test the infant. He would take the gold if he was a king, the incense if a priest, the myrrh if a doctor. Thus as humans are wont to do, the magi meant to classify the child. Confounding them, Jesus took all three."[4]

He took all three. Christ is "all in all" (1 Corinthians 15:28).

In another fanciful story, it's said that "the three gifts of the magi came from a treasure cavern that had been filled by Adam himself from the wealth of paradise."[5]

Adam himself put these three gifts on layaway for Jesus, thousands of years before that first Christmas. And the wise men, granted magical access to these treasures, stopped by the cave on their way.

This is exactly the kind of story that tends to snowball through the years, gathering mass as it rolls downhill, until it flattens Matthew's philosophers into avatars of incalculable wealth and power.

If only these wise men could be tracked back to their homelands, the thinking goes, then their wealth—paradisiacal treasure caves and all—could be ours!

"Before 1480," Trexler says, "the search for the homelands of the magi was a matter of religious curiosity." But all this changed "with the discovery of the extra-European world in the following century." With entirely new continents ripe for subjugation and exploration, "some explorers became convinced that to discover the homelands of the magi was to capture for oneself inestimable wealth in spices and precious metals," such that, "to an extent little imagined by previous historians, the search for El Dorado, for the seven cities of Cibola, and indeed later for Shangri-la, is part of the search for the magi."[6]

Columbus bought this bedtime story lock, stock, and barrel. "There can be no doubt," Trexler says, that "Columbus structured his expectations in this part of the world, inter alia, around the presumed homelands of the three kings." In fact, "in addition to direct references to the magi, the admiral expressed confidence that he had found the fabled city or land of Ophir, a great source of gold in the ancient world and thus often associated with the first of the three kings."[7]

Did the wise men have families? Did they love their wives and children? Or were they monks—eunuchs, celibates, ascetics—locked in lonely towers with their books and charts?

Did the wise men welcome commotion and interruptions? Or did they shudder at the racket made by a child?

Were they amazed by Jesus because they'd never seen a child before? Or were they amazed because Jesus, the Son of God, was just like their own?

Matthew doesn't say.

Were all Matthew's magoi men?

Matthew doesn't say.

Probably.

Though, intriguingly, Trexler devotes a dozen pages to examining a wide range of traditional Christian paintings that, over time, chose to depict the third wise man with increasingly feminine features, manners, and attire.[8]

I have a Christmas photo, also from 1984, of what counts in my family as an exotic and legendary gift.

The photo shows just this: a chimpanzee sitting sidesaddle.

A sawhorse, wrapped in Christmas paper, is centered on the hearth of our fireplace. A saddle sits atop the sawhorse. And my stuffed animal, Ruth, rides atop the saddle. Apart from two red stockings hanging from the mantel, this accounts for everything in the photo.

The saddle is a Christmas gift for my mother. Ever since she was a child, she'd wanted a horse. So when we moved into that farmhouse, my father built a barn, picked out a saddle, and bought my mom a giant red Quarter Horse, just two years old. The horse had been bred to show but had scarred his leg as a foal. Still, he was strong and beautiful. His name was J.R. And my mom loved him more than most anything but us.

My dad, though, went back to school and six years later got a new job on the other side of the state. So we sold the farm and the horse and moved into what was easily the most beautiful house my parents ever owned. My mom never cared for it.

Twenty years after my dad first bought my mom this horse, he bought her another. Or, rather, he bought her the same horse again. My father had to play detective. He had to cross his fingers that the horse was still alive and then track him down. J.R. was old and he'd passed through several hands, but my dad found him, brought him home, and gave him to my mother as an anniversary present.

My mom took care of J.R. for two more years until he died. She and the horse had both given up on galloping through the countryside, but she visited him all the time. She brushed his long mane and whispered secrets in his ears and fed him apples until they ran out of time.

My mom, it has always seemed to me, was unaccountably fond of the modest gray house they lived in at the time.

Picture my mom in the barn with this horse.

How old is she? Sixty-one? Or six?

How quiet is her mind? How much does she feel of what the horse feels?

"Literally from the time they're born," Gopnik says, "children are empathic. They identify with other people and recognize that their own feelings are shared by others."[9] It's not hard to see that "even very young babies are paying careful attention to other people. They pay particularly close attention to the contingencies between their own actions and emotions and those of others." In short, "the baby notices that when he smiles, Mom smiles back."[10] This kind of empathy is so powerful, Gopnik argues, "it's possible that babies literally don't see a difference between their own pain and the pain of others."[11]

This claim may, at first, sound strange. But such experiences are both common and contagious. Parents, primed by their children to experience the world in a childlike way, often experience the same thing. "Parents are on the other side of those intimate early face-to-face interactions. And it sure doesn't feel as if we react to our baby's pain simply because we want to feel better ourselves. Instead, the pain just pulls on our heartstrings directly. I literally feel my baby's pain with as much intensity as my own pain. The impulse to soothe my baby is just as automatic and immediate as my impulse to soothe myself."[12]

Do you want to be born again? Spend time with children.

Do you need faith? Find a baby to hold.

Do you need to repent and change your mind? Play make-believe with a child.

Do you need Spirit? Respond to someone else's pain as immediately as your own.

"And they brought young children to him, that he should touch them: and his disciples rebuked those that brought them. But when Jesus saw it, he was much displeased, and said unto them, Suffer the little children to come unto me, and forbid them not: for of such is the kingdom of God." And then "he took them up in his arms, put his hands upon them, and blessed them" (Mark 10:13–14, 16).

How displeased is Jesus?

Wrapped up in my story, hunkered down behind the walls of my grown-up "self," a lot of what I care about and worry about as an adult is straight nonsense. It's bunkum. It's moonshine. It's baloney. It's malarkey. It's petty, trivial, and utterly beside the point.

How much of what I do and think every day is nonsense? How much of it is utterly beside the point? How much, even, of what I think of as "religion"—just like those misguided disciples—fits this same bill?

How much time do I spend ushering children away?

The line between sense and nonsense is bright.

If it involves loving the way children do, it matters.

But if it doesn't involve this pure love, it's "nothing."

"If I speak in the tongues of men and of angels, but I do not have love, I am a noisy gong or a clanging cymbal" (1 Corinthians 13:1, NET).

Or even "if I give away everything I own . . . but do not have love," then I'm still nothing (1 Corinthians 13:3, NET).

Or even more, even if I "know all mysteries and all knowledge, and if I have all faith so that I can remove mountains, but do not have love, I am nothing" (1 Corinthians 13:2, NET).

"Love is patient, love is kind. It does not envy, it does not boast, it is not proud. It does not dishonor others, it is not self-seeking, it is not easily angered, it keeps no record of wrongs. Love does not delight in evil but rejoices with the truth. It always protects, always trusts, always hopes, always perseveres. Love never fails" (1 Corinthians 13:4–8, NIV).

Love doesn't envy. It keeps no record of wrongs. It always trusts. It never fails.

The wise men, I suspect, weren't rich or powerful. Indifferent to such nonsense, they loved books. They loved the stars. And, of course, they loved their many, many children.

They didn't travel for years as sad, nomadic bachelors

with only camels for company. They brought everyone along. All the wives, all the grandparents, all the children, all the cousins, all the horses.

They made jokes and raced around the tents and told stories by the fire. They sang and they danced. They named the constellations. They shared what they had, offered sacrifices to their God, and prayed both day and night. They played and loved the whole way there and then, again, the whole way back.

And when they finally arrived in Bethlehem, no one could bear to wait outside. Everyone wanted to see the child. And so everyone in the whole caravan squeezed into that tiny room to greet the Christ Child, packed in so tight they might as well have been one body.

And Jesus smiled at the sight of them.

And everyone felt his love.

And everyone felt what everyone else was feeling.

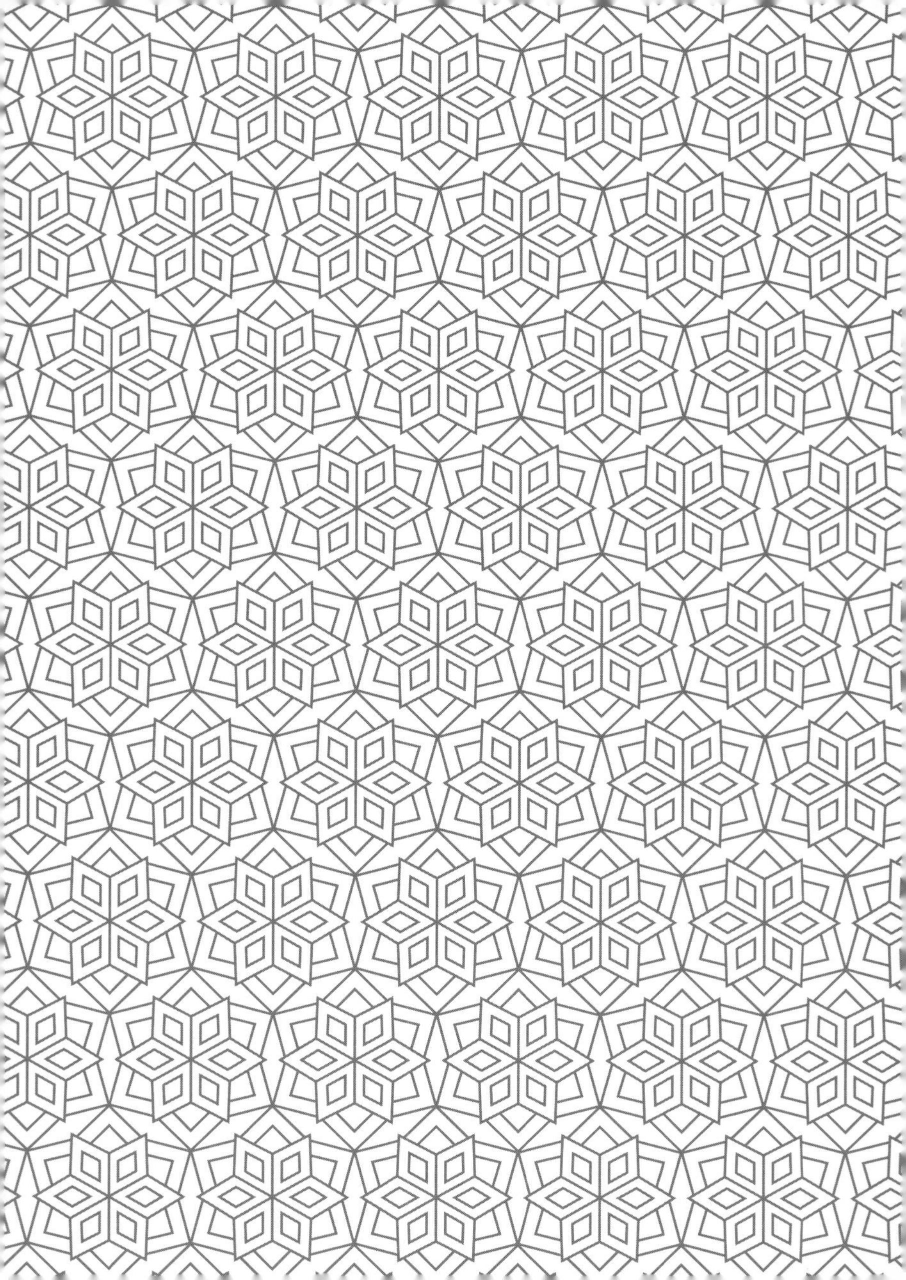

Conclusion

In the photo, I'm a child again. It's Christmas.

I'm lying flat on my back in the snow, my nose and cheeks red. I've been tackled by my father. I've still got a snowball in one hand. I'm rolling my eyes heavenward, tongue out, hamming it up for the photographer, surely my mom. I'm wearing gray snow boots with a blue stripe and dark snow pants with zippered legs. The boots and pants are caked with damp snow, like I've already been outside all afternoon. My puffy coat is blue with red sleeves. The hood is up, partially hiding my yellow beanie—woolen, askew—emblazoned with a Pittsburgh Steelers logo. Every kid within three hundred miles is wearing a yellow beanie with a Pittsburgh Steelers logo.

I'm guessing I must be six or seven.

We're at the top of the hill above the farmhouse. Everything is covered in a half foot of snow. From where we are, the hill slopes steeply for about fifty yards, levels out around the house, and then rolls steeply for another fifty yards down toward the creek where, in a few years, the horse barn will be. In this photo, at the top of the hill, we're backed by a free-standing, white brick building I assume was originally built as a one-car garage. My father, though, has gotten the idea to repurpose this building as a barn for a half dozen cattle. A dilapidated grain silo looms behind the garage, but it's not visible in the picture. A length of hose is loosely coiled near the spigot. The weather looks cold, but not bitterly so.

My father has me pinned to the ground. He's using one hand to cushion my fall and the other to restrain my throwing arm. He's looking at the photographer. He's not wearing a shirt and tie, but he's not dressed to play in the snow either. Rather, he's wearing a version of his chore clothes—blue jeans, laced boots, a rough canvas-colored jacket—like he'd been meaning to feed the cows when we bushwhacked him. He's smiling. He seems relieved to not be feeding the cows. (The cows can wait.) He seems relieved to be playing with us. The oversized transition lenses of his glasses are dark in the bright sun. Their frames are rounded on the bottom with a single bar flat across the top. Like me, he's wearing a beanie, pulled down over his ears. This beanie is light brown with a dark pom. My grandmother, my mother's mother, knitted this cap. My father, as always, is clean-shaven. He looks young and strong—much younger than I am now. He's got dreams. He's got plans. He loves us.

The photo's background is washed out by the snow's uniform glare. But if you look closely, you can see that the snow behind us isn't just more snow. Rather, it's snow that kids have spent hours gathering and packing, gathering and packing, to form the semicircular, three-foot-high wall of an imposing snow fort. (Nota bene: A thin smudge of dark hair is barely visible behind these battlements—my little sister, again.) Provisioned with piles of ready-made snowballs and positioned as it is at the top of the hill, the fort's strategic advantages would have been significant. Seeing the odds stacked against him, my father must have rushed the fort, braving our wild volley, to claim me as his first casualty.

So, here I am: laid out on the ground, wrapped in his arms.

All in all, the scene is biblical.

The son, laid low, is taken again into the bosom of the father.

To become a child again—to be converted and saved—I'll need to recover that child's mind. I'll need all of his awe, imagination, and love. I'll need to be attuned, amplified, and decentered.

But still, vital as this is, it's not enough—or even desirable—for me to simply become a child again. It's not enough for me to just be a son. The world is full of people who've never grown up. To be saved, to be a disciple of Christ, I must learn how to be *both* an adult and a child. I must learn how to be both a father and a son.

And this is the mystery of mysteries.

This is the mystery of godliness itself: how to be both. How to become an adult, tempered by age and experience, and, nonetheless, see the world through a child's eyes. How to pair all the skill, strength, and wisdom of an adult with all the wonder, creativity, and empathy of a child.

How, simply, to live like Jesus.

But how? How can a man be born when he is old?

"Lord, how is it done?" (Enos 1:7).

Abinadi's explanation of Christmas—of Godhood joined with childhood—is one of the best. In Mosiah 15, he's trying to explain, with his own life in the balance, how the Father and the Son are, in fact, "one God" (Mosiah 15:4).

The trick to following Abinadi's explanation is to see how, rather than using the titles of Father and Son to name two different people, he applies both titles to Christ. He's not commenting (confusedly) on the nature of the Godhead, he's explaining (clearly) the work of atonement.

Christ, he says, is both "the Father, because he was conceived by the power of God; and the Son, because of the flesh; thus becoming the Father and Son" (Mosiah 15:3). Or, as he reframes this in the verses that follow: Christ is the Father because of the Spirit and the Son because of the flesh, with "the flesh becoming subject to the Spirit, or the Son to the Father, being one God" (Mosiah 15:5).

This is the model: flesh becomes subject to Spirit, the Son becomes subject to the Father, and thus they become "one God."

The problem is that, though I must become a child again, I can't do this by going back to the beginning. I can't, as Nicodemus points out, reenter the womb and be born again. I can't wish myself into a second childhood. And, what's more, I certainly can't wish myself onto some other path than this one—this mortal path, where, regardless of what I want, I will grow up, I will grow old, and I will die.

I can't wish myself into believing those sleigh bells were real.

Just the opposite. To become a child again, I must keep going. I must push through to the end, all the way through to the end of my life—and then, in Christ, I must keep going.

For me, the only door leading back to birth is death.

The only way back is through.

I must worship again at the Christ Child's feet. I must follow his star.

But this new star, blazing in the darkness, is the sign of his cross.

To be reborn and become a child again, I must be "crucified with Christ" (Galatians 2:20). I must be "crucified with him, that the body of sin might be destroyed" (Romans 6:6). I must let Christ draw me to him on the cross so that, as he tells the Nephites, "as I have been lifted up by men even so should men be lifted up by the Father" (3 Nephi 27:14).

To be raised "in the likeness of his resurrection," he and I must first be "planted together in the likeness of his death" (Romans 6:5).

This path—with Christ, through the cross—is childlike in its foolishness.

It pulls against the grain of everything the world has ever taught me: that everything is about me, that I'm the hero of my own story, that happiness depends on getting what I want, that I should run from suffering, especially when it's not my own, that I should avoid, at all costs, loss and death and sacrifice.

But this, Paul insists, is not the gospel. Yes, "the preaching of the cross is to them that perish foolishness; but unto us which are saved it is the power of God" (1 Corinthians 1:18).

In Christ, God has made foolish the wisdom of this world.

In Christ, God has turned this world upside down, given it a hard shake, and set everything aswirl.

"But God hath chosen the foolish things of the world to confound the wise; and God hath chosen the weak things of the world to confound the things which are mighty; and base things of the world, and things which are despised, hath God chosen, yea, and things which are not, to bring to nought things that are" (1 Corinthians 1:27–28).

What better example of a disciple—of a "weak thing," of a foolish thing—than a child?

Abinadi preaches this same gospel: the Father and the Son become one God only by way of the cross.

"Thus the flesh becoming subject to the Spirit, or the Son to the Father, being one God, suffereth temptation, and yieldeth not to the temptation, but suffereth himself to be mocked, and scourged, and cast out, and disowned by his people. . . . Yea, even so he shall be led, crucified, and slain, the flesh becoming subject even unto death, the will of the Son being swallowed up in the will of the Father. And thus God breaketh the bands of death" (Mosiah 15:5, 7–8).

This is the path.

This is the way of the cross: if I want to be both an adult

and a child, both a father and a son, then I must bear suffering and difficulty without yielding to them.

God's will must become my will.

In Eastern Christianity, Mary is called *theotokos*—often rendered in English as "Mother of God" or "God-bearer."

Mary is a God-bearer.

Bearing the Son of God in her womb, Mary is both parent and child. They are one flesh. She carries God within her *as* a child. She literally gives her life—blood and iron, bone and marrow—for the life of that child.

Her life is swallowed up in the work of giving him life.

Could there be a better image for how to be *both* parent and child than Mary, God-bearer, bearing God as a child inside her?

God's will becomes my will when I finally start trusting his will more than my own.

This is faith: to trust God like children trust their parents.

Trusting God, I stop filtering reality through the narrow aperture of my own desires. I stop fixating on my sour fantasies. I stop locking all my doors and hoarding all my gifts as treasures.

Trusting God, I have an epiphany.

I imagine something new.

I give life to something new.

I love.

Do I believe in Christmas? Can I think like a child? Have I shared the mind of Christ?

Do I trust God's word that this world *is* good? And do I obey his command to always and only respond to this world with more good? Even if this world will never be what I wanted?

When I look at this world, do I see what God sees? Do I feel what God feels?

It's Christmas morning.

I wake up early, too early, excited for the day.

And I find myself wanting to believe in the magic of Christmas.

How is it done?

It's still dark. The heat hasn't kicked on yet and the house is cold. I'm burrowed in my blankets, waiting, listening. I listen to the wind rattle the window. I listen to my brother snoring. I listen to the old house creaking. I listen to my heart beating.

The silence deepens.

There are no sleigh bells.

My mind swells wide. I lose track of my story. I forget what I want and trust what's given. The floor, my blankets, the wind, the windows—these are my body. These are my own skin and bones. I can feel the house breathing. I can feel what the house feels. I can feel my brother dreaming. I love all of it.

I have the mind of a child.

I have the mind of Christ.

This is Christmas.

Notes

INTRODUCTION

1. Alison Gopnik, *The Philosophical Baby: What Children's Minds Tell Us About Truth, Love, and the Meaning of Life* (New York: Farrar, Straus, and Giroux, 2009), 4.
2. Gopnik, 9.
3. Gopnik, 14.
4. Gopnik, 5.

CHAPTER ONE: AWE

1. This text is taken directly from Luke 1:46–55, though the clarifying line breaks are my own.
2. Alison Gopnik, *The Philosophical Baby: What Children's Minds Tell Us About Truth, Love, and the Meaning of Life* (New York: Farrar, Straus, and Giroux, 2009), 125.
3. Gopnik, 239.
4. Gopnik, 119.
5. Gopnik, 117.

6. Gopnik, 129.
7. Gopnik, 112.
8. Shunryu Suzuki, *Zen Mind, Beginner's Mind* (Boston: Shambhala, 2006), 2, 24.
9. Richard C. Trexler, *The Journey of the Magi: Meanings in History of a Christian Story* (Princeton: Princeton University Press, 1997), 9.
10. Trexler, 9.
11. Trexler, 26.

CHAPTER TWO: IMAGINATION

1. History, 1838–1856, volume E-1 [1 July 1843–30 April 1844], pp. 1866–1867, *The Joseph Smith Papers*, accessed November 20, 2023, https://www.josephsmithpapers.org/paper-summary/history-1838-1856-volume-e-1-1-july-1843-30-april-1844/127.
2. Alison Gopnik, *The Philosophical Baby: What Children's Minds Tell Us About Truth, Love, and the Meaning of Life* (New York: Farrar, Straus, and Giroux, 2009), 28.
3. Gopnik, 240.
4. Gopnik, 11.
5. Gopnik, 73.
6. John Henry Hopkins Jr., "We Three Kings." For the full text, see https://en.wikipedia.org/wiki/We_Three_Kings.
7. Richard C. Trexler, *The Journey of the Magi: Meanings in History of a Christian Story* (Princeton: Princeton University Press, 1997), 53. The history associated with this particular example of Christian syncretism is blurry, fragmentary, and complex. For a fuller account of how these traditions simultaneously developed and unfolded across a wide variety of Christian cultures and historical eras, see the whole of chapters 2 and 3 of Trexler's *The Journey of the Magi*.

8. Hopkins, "We Three Kings."
9. Trexler, 69.
10. Trexler, 77; the emphasis is mine.
11. See Trexler, 180.
12. Trexler, 176.
13. Trexler, 176.
14. Henry B. Eyring, "Gifts of Peace," 2016 Christmas devotional, https://www.churchofjesuschrist.org/study/broadcasts/first-presidency-christmas-devotional/2016/12/gifts-of-peace?lang=eng; the emphasis is mine.
15. Gopnik, 71.
16. Gopnik, 32.

CHAPTER THREE: LOVE

1. Alison Gopnik, *The Philosophical Baby: What Children's Minds Tell Us About Truth, Love, and the Meaning of Life* (New York: Farrar, Straus, and Giroux, 2009), 153.
2. Gopnik, 138.
3. Gopnik, 147, 17, 145, 149.
4. Richard C. Trexler, *The Journey of the Magi: Meanings in History of a Christian Story* (Princeton: Princeton University Press, 1997), 40–41.
5. Trexler, 39.
6. Trexler, 124.
7. Trexler, 138.
8. See Trexler, 107–119.
9. Gopnik, 204.
10. Gopnik, 181.
11. Gopnik, 207.
12. Gopnik, 208.

About the Author

Photo by Jennifer Griffith

ADAM S. MILLER is a professor of philosophy at Collin College in McKinney, Texas. He earned a BA in comparative literature from Brigham Young University and an MA and PhD in philosophy from Villanova University. He is the author of more than a dozen books, including *Letters to a Young Mormon, Original Grace,* and (co-authored with Rosalynde Welch) *Seven Gospels*. He and his wife, Gwen, have three children.